ORANGES

FARM TO MARKET

Jason Cooper

Rourke Publications, Inc.
Vero Beach, Florida 32964

Edited by Pamela J.P. Schroeder

PHOTO CREDITS
All photos © Lynn M. Stone

Library of Congress Cataloging-in-Publication Data
Cooper, Jason, 1942-
    Oranges / by Jason Cooper.
      p. cm. — (Farm to market)
    Summary: Describes how North American oranges are grown, harvested, processed, and shipped to consumers.
    ISBN 0-86625-621-0
    1. Orange—Juvenile literature. 2. Orange products—Juvenile literature. 3. Orange—United States—Juvenile literature. 4. Orange products—United States—Juvenile literature.
[1. Orange.] I. Title. II. Series: Cooper, Jason, 1942-
Farm to market.
SB370.O7C65 1997
634'.31—dc21
                                97-13232
                                    CIP
                                    AC

Printed in the USA

TABLE OF CONTENTS

ORANGES

Oranges are sold in stores, but they grow on trees. Before they reach stores, many oranges have had a long journey.

Like their cousins, lemons and grapefruit, oranges are from warm climates.

They grow on rows of trees in groves, or orchards. By late winter or early spring, 1,200 oranges may hang from the branches of just one tree. An orange grove is an orangutan's dreamland!

Oranges belong to the citrus family of fruits. Citrus are known for their firm **peels** (PEELZ) and pulpy, juicy insides.

A Florida orange tree in April is loaded with ripe fruit and white blossoms.

KINDS OF ORANGES

Most oranges grown in the United States look like orange-colored baseballs. Some oranges, though, are oval. Blood oranges have pink or red fruit and peels. Hamlin oranges have yellow fruit and peels.

American growers plant several varieties, or kinds, of oranges. Some varieties, such as the Hamlin, ripen early in the season. Others, like the popular Valencias, ripen later.

Valencias are the most common oranges in America because they have the most juice.

Raindrops bathe Valencia oranges and the tree's dark green leaves. Orange trees need rain, but they don't like "wet feet."

WHERE ORANGES GROW

Orange trees do best in climates with warm summers and cool winters. However, temperatures below freezing can kill trees and hurt the oranges.

Eight of every 10 American oranges grow in Florida. Most of the groves are in the central and southern part of the state.

California is second in growing oranges. Arizona and Texas also grow oranges for market.

The sandy soil and warmth of south central Florida are great for orange groves.

PLANTING ORANGE TREES

Orange trees will grow from seeds, but that is not how orange farmers grow them. Instead, farmers give young trees a "head start."

Farmers join a tiny cutting from one tree with a young root system, called **rootstock** (ROOT stahk).

The rootstock may be from any kind of citrus tree. Farmers look for rootstock that will grow well where they are planting. Many Florida orange trees have lemon rootstocks.

The "new" tree, however, will grow oranges, not lemons. By using rootstock, a farmer can have oranges in just three or four years. Growing a tree from seed might take 15 years!

Young orange trees grow from rootstocks. They are wrapped for protection against freezing.

11

Fresh from the farm, trucks deliver oranges to a packinghouse and juice-processing plant in central Florida.

Oranges are washed as they tumble along a processing line at a packinghouse. Later, the best oranges will be given a light coat of wax for protection.

GROWING ORANGES

Orange trees have many enemies, including ants, scale insects, heart rot, foot rot, and mites. Winter cold can wipe out entire groves.

Protecting the grove is always a battle. Orange farmers fight insects with chemical sprays. They use other chemicals, called **herbicides** (ER buh sydz), to kill plant pests.

In cold weather, farmers use blasts of hot air and warm mist to protect the trees' fruit and leaves.

Mist hoses give trees moisture during the dry summer. During cold spells, the warmer-than-air mist helps protect trees.

HARVESTING

Each kind of orange ripens at a different time. The Florida harvest usually begins in December and goes into April.

Farmers pick almost all their oranges by hand. Mechanical pickers can hurt fruit and branches.

Orange pickers climb ladders and drop their oranges into big sacks. As a sack fills, the picker puts the oranges into a box on the ground. Trucks take away the filled boxes.

A picker in Florida fills a sack with 45 pounds (20.5 kg) of oranges before climbing down the ladder and emptying the load.

PROCESSING

Trucks deliver oranges to **processing** (PRAH sess ing) plants, or **packinghouses** (PA king hous ez). In the United States, three of every four oranges are processed, or changed, into juice. Packinghouses gather, sort, and ship fresh oranges.

Orange juice may be bottled, canned, or put into cartons. Some of it is quick-frozen.

Oranges that will be sold whole are processed differently. They are sorted, washed, and dried. Some are sprayed with a gas that makes the orange color look better. Then they are covered with a light skin of wax.

Workers sort oranges at a packinghouse. The best fruit will be boxed. Less-than-perfect fruit will be juiced.

ORANGE PRODUCTS

Refrigerated trucks and train cars haul oranges and juice from the processing plants. They deliver them to supermarkets or large food **distributors** (dih STRIHB u terz). Distributors sell to food stores.

A small part of each orange crop is used in jams, jellies, candy, soft drinks, and baking goods.

Orange peels are ground up for cattle feed and oil. Orange oil is added to some paints, perfumes, and baking mixes.

Oranges are made into several food products.

ORANGES AS FOOD

Orange juice is tasty because of its natural sugars. More important, orange juice has **nutrients** (NU tree ents) such as vitamin C, a B vitamin, and potassium.

Among other things, vitamin C helps the body keep infection away, heal scrapes and cuts, and build bones.

Potassium helps keep our body cells healthy. Folic acid, a B vitamin, helps body cells grow.

Whole oranges, with their flesh or pulp, give us fiber. Fiber helps the body digest food.

Glossary

distributor (dih STRIHB u ter) — a person or place that gathers products, such as oranges, in large numbers and re-sells them to stores

herbicide (ER buh syd) — chemicals used to kill plant pests

nutrient (NU tree ent) — any of several "good" substances that the body needs for health, growth, and energy; vitamins and minerals

packinghouse (PA king hous) — a place that sorts, packages, and sells large amounts of whole fruit

peel (PEEL) — the skin on some kinds of fruit, such as oranges and grapefruits

processing (PRAH sess ing) — the steps to prepare fresh fruit or meat for market

rootstock (ROOT stahk) — the root system and stem of a tree that is joined with a bud from another tree

INDEX